IF FC

Greater Than a Tourist Book Series Reviews from Readers

I think the series is wonderful and beneficial for tourists to get information before visiting the city. -Seckin Zumbul, Izmir Turkey

I am a world traveler who has read many trip guides but this one really made a difference for me. I would call it a heartfelt creation of a local guide expert instead of just a guide. -Susy, Isla Holbox, Mexico

New to the area like me, this is a must have! -Joe, Bloomington, USA

This is a good series that gets down to it when looking for things to do at your destination without

i

having to read a novel for just a few ideas. -Rachel, Monterey, USA

Good information to have to plan my trip to this destination. -Pennie Farrell, Mexico

Great ideas for a port day. -Mary Martin USA

Aptly titled, you won't just be a tourist after reading this book. You'll be greater than a tourist! -Alan Warner, Grand Rapids, USA

Even though I only have three days to spend in San Miguel in an upcoming visit, I will use the author's suggestions to guide some of my time there. An easy read - with chapters named to guide me in directions I want to go. -Robert Catapano, USA

Great insights from a local perspective! Useful information and a very good value! -Sarah, USA

This series provides an in-depth experience through the eyes of a local. Reading these series will help you to travel the city in with confidence and it'll make your journey a unique one. -Andrew Teoh, Ipoh, Malaysia

>TOURIST

GREATER THAN A TOURIST – SANTIAGO DE QUERETARO MEXICO

50 Travel Tips from a Local

Veronica Rudich

Greater Than a Tourist- Santiago De Queretaro Mexico Copyright © 2018 by CZYK Publishing LLC. All Rights Reserved.

All rights reserved. No part of this book may be reproduced in any form or by any electronic or mechanical means including information storage and retrieval systems, without permission in writing from the author. The only exception is by a reviewer, who may quote short excerpts in a review.

Cover designed by: Ivana Stamenkovic
Cover Image: https://pixabay.com/en/avenue-queretaro-mexico-170390/

CZYK
PUBLISHING

Greater Than a Tourist
Visit our website at www.GreaterThanaTourist.com

Lock Haven, PA
All rights reserved.
ISBN: 9781717749581

>TOURIST
50 TRAVEL TIPS FROM A LOCAL

BOOK DESCRIPTION

Are you excited about planning your next trip?

Do you want to try something new?

Would you like some guidance from a local?

If you answered yes to any of these questions, then this Greater Than a Tourist book is for you.

Greater Than a Tourist- Santiago De Queretaro Mexico by Veronica Rudich offers the inside scoop on Queretaro. Most travel books tell you how to travel like a tourist. Although there is nothing wrong with that, as part of the Greater Than a Tourist series, this book will give you travel tips from someone who has lived at your next travel destination.

In these pages, you will discover advice that will help you throughout your stay. This book will not tell you exact addresses or store hours but instead will give you excitement and knowledge from a local that you may not find in other smaller print travel books.

Travel like a local. Slow down, stay in one place, and get to know the people and the culture. By the time you finish this book, you will be eager and prepared to travel to your next destination.

TABLE OF CONTENTS

BOOK DESCRIPTION
TABLE OF CONTENTS
DEDICATION
ABOUT THE AUTHOR
HOW TO USE THIS BOOK
FROM THE PUBLISHER
OUR STORY
WELCOME TO
> TOURIST
INTRODUCTION
1. The Correct Name
2. Best Time to Come
3. How to Get to Queretaro
4. Where to Stay
5. Mexican Food
6. Street Tacos in Queretaro
7. Homemade Ice-cream.
8. It is not Spicy
9. Dinner and a View
10. Best Margarita
11. Cheese and Wine Routes
12. Peña de Bernal
13. Piramid
14. El Mirador

15. Los Arcos
16. Tequisquiapan
17. Parque Bicentenario
18. City Myths
19. All the Bars
20. Gracias a Dios
21. Downtown Oasis
22. Fairs
23. Foreigners' Parade
24. Foreigners' Festival
25. Queretaro's Comic-Con
26. Museo Regional
27. Handicraft Fairs and Stores
28. Dolls
29. Dia de los Muertos
30. Mexican Independence Day Celebration
31. Silent Procession
32. Holidays are for Everyone
33. Movies
34. Sierra Gorda
35. Escondido Place
36. Golf in Queretaro
37. Weekend Rest for Everybody
38. Public Transport in Queretaro
39. Uber vs Taxi in Queretaro
40. Rental Car

>TOURIST

41. Greetings
42. Foreigners
43. Gringos
44. Communication
45. If You Need Help with Spanish
46. If you don't Feel Well
47. Things You Should Not Forget
48. People Asking for Money
49. Explore Neighbouring States
50. Best Places to Take Pictures

TOP REASONS TO BOOK THIS TRIP
50 THINGS TO KNOW ABOUT PACKING LIGHT FOR TRAVEL
Packing and Planning Tips
Travel Questions
Travel Bucket List
NOTES

\>TOURIST

DEDICATION

This book is dedicated to my husband, who took me to Mexico and suggested living in the beautifil city of Queretaro, where we have found your home and joy.

ABOUT THE AUTHOR

Veronika Rudich is a translator from Ukraine, who now lives in Santiago de Queretato, Mexico. Before moving to this beautiful city she also tried living in Celaya, which didn't turn out to be a great place.

Veronica loves travelling, she has visited several countries in Europe and many places in the USA, where she met her husband. She thought it was her last adventure untill he suggested moving to Mexico. It seemed like a crazy idea at first. Now, after more than a year living, working and travelling in Mexico, they both think it was one of the best decisions they have ever taken.

Veronica loves sharing her emmotions and experience through her hobby – writing. So, as you can see, this is the reason why this book was writted.

>TOURIST

HOW TO USE THIS BOOK

The Greater Than a Tourist book series was written by someone who has lived in an area for over three months. The goal of this book is to help travelers either dream or experience different locations by providing opinions from a local. The author has made suggestions based on their own experiences. Please do your own research before traveling to the area in case the suggested places are unavailable.

FROM THE PUBLISHER

Traveling can be one of the most important parts of a person's life. The anticipation and memories that you have are some of the best. As a publisher of the Greater Than a Tourist book series, as well as the popular 50 Things to Know book series, we strive to help you learn about new places, spark your imagination, and inspire you. Wherever you are and whatever you do I wish you safe, fun, and inspiring travel.

Lisa Rusczyk Ed. D.
CZYK Publishing

OUR STORY

Traveling is a passion of the "Greater than a Tourist" series creator. Lisa studied abroad in college, and for their honeymoon Lisa and her husband toured Europe. During her travels to Malta, an older man tried to give her some advice based on his own experience living on the island since he was a young boy. She was not sure if she should talk to the stranger but was interested in his advice. When traveling to some places she was wary to talk to locals because she was afraid that they weren't being genuine. Through her travels, Lisa learned how much locals had to share with tourists. Lisa created the "Greater Than a Tourist" book series to help connect people with locals. A topic that locals are very passionate about sharing.

>TOURIST

WELCOME TO
> TOURIST

INTRODUCTION

"The use of traveling is to regulate imagination with reality, and instead of thinking of how things may be, see them as they are."
– Samuel Johnson

In many situations we think about Mexico as a paradise escape for our vacation, we think about its beaches with white sand and warm transparent water... On the other hand we all also know stereotypes about Mexico. If you are a thinking person, you understand that more than a half of stereotypes about any country is not true. The best way to prove this is to go and see everything with your own eyes. To see that Mexico is not only about resorts and Mayas, that there is so much history and culture hidden right in the middle of the counrty, waiting for you to explore and experience it.

One of the best places for such experience is Santiago de Queretaro. Now it is bustling and quick-growing city, but it has a lot to tell you about its past. This is the place where lots of decisions that led Mexico to independence have been made. On top of that, in 1996 the historic center of Queretaro was declared a World Heritage Site by the UNESCO. Queretaro has been recognized as the metro area with the best quality of life and as the safest city in Mexico. .

>TOURIST

1. THE CORRECT NAME

The capital and the largest city in Queretaro state has its official name – Santiago de Queretaro. The city is also known as Queretaro city or simply Queretaro. You may hear people say any of this names, remeber that they always refer to the city. If they mean the state, they will say «estado de Queretaro».

When you are looking for a place and using Google maps, or other apps, it will be stated there that your place is located in, for example, Corregidora, Juriquilla,Centro Sur, Centro Historico, Santa Rosa or Pueblito. These are now parts of Queretaro city, but they were separate towns before. With the flow of time they grew and became a part of Queretaro. So, when you see something like this in your directions, don't worry, it is still in Queretaro, you don't have to go to another city.

2. BEST TIME TO COME

Mexico is well known for its sunny weather, however, you may think your vacation is ruined, if you come here during the rainy season. Sometimes it is difficult to say exactly when it starts and finishes.

Rainy season runs approximately from May/June till October, sometimes November. These days may slightly differ each year. Rainy season does not sound fun at all, but you need to remember that even though it rains nearly every day, it does not take more than two or three hours. In some rare occasions it can rain for the whole evening, but you will have your morning and afternoon rain-free.

So even if you find yousefl in Mexico during this period of the year, do not get upset, you will have time to enjoy the country before or after the rain. The only thing you have to do is to plan you day taking rain into the consideration.

3. HOW TO GET TO QUERETARO

Every adventure starts with getting to the place you think it should start. In our case it is Queretaro city. Getting here will not be difficult as Queretaro has its own airport, which is less than an hour away from the city. However, If you are flying from overseas, you probably will need to make a transfer in Mexico City or Cancun airport. Note, that there are buses that depart from Mexico City to Queretaro every hour. If you decide to go by bus, it will take you about 4 hours and it will be just a little less expensive than a plane, but travelling by plane takes only one hour, in some cases an hour and a half.

4. WHERE TO STAY

Once you are in Queretaro you will not have a problem with accomodation. There is a great deal of hotels and airbnb, they are located in every part of the city. Here we have hotels that are well-known in the world and also Mexican hotels and hostels. You will find multiple hotels in the downtown area. Most likely they will have a view over one of the city parks or squares. Not too far from downtown, in front of the city park Alameda, you can find several nice hotels. One of them even has a rooftop bar with jacuzzi.

I would not advise you to stay in a motel. Mostly they charge you per hour or per 8 hours, which may be unusual. The reason why they do it is that Mexicans tend to use motels to make love.

5. MEXICAN FOOD

Mexican Food is special in many different ways, so when you come here make sure you are not missing out. There are several things that you should try such as dishes with nopal (cactus), pozole (soup), chicken with mole (sauce made from chillli peppers, spices and chocolate), elote, chicharron (deep-fried pork skeen).

To try Mexican food you can go to such restaurants as San Miguelito or La Palapa, there are more restaurants of Mexican cuisine that you can visit, but those two are known for being the best. Another option is to buy some food from street vendors. There is a great deal of them during festivals and fairs. Early in the morning there are food sellers on the street providing rushing people with there breakfast.

6. STREET TACOS IN QUERETARO

Every Mexican loves tacos, they are unbelievably good. You will notice how popular they are – there are taco stands and tiny taco restaurants everywhere you go. Yes, they don't look very fancy, but it does not mean that they are bad. If you are afraid to buy tacos on the street, you can go to a taco restaurant called El Pata. There are several of them in the city.

Also note that tacos come in various size. Some can be bigger, other can be smaller. The way tacos are served differs also. You may get one tortilla per taco or two. Some cooks put a piece of pineapple in each taco, some give you chopped pineapples in a bowl. Same thing with onion and cilantro. This is why if you see this differences, don't think that there is something wrong. There is no establish standard of how tacos should be served.

7. HOMEMADE ICE-CREAM.

When in Queretaro, you will notice small ice-cream shops (especially in the downtown area). Mostly they are run by families and their ice-cream is homemade or it is made in there shop. This ice-cream is not expencive and tastes dedlicious. This shops can offer you unsual flavours, for example marzipan, cheese, red wine, rom and raisins, tequila, guava, sapote, etc. Besides for ice-cream you can also buy here some refreshing Mexican drinks.

8. IT IS NOT SPICY

Mostly every Mexican traditional dish is spicy. Be careful if you are not a chilli lover and remember that Mexicans got used to eating spicy food. They use chilli, jalapeño, poblano or habanero depending on the dish. Therefore, if you ask whether the food is hot or not, it will be difficult for them to say. If a Mexican says that something is not spicy at all, there is a chance that it is still a little spicy. If he says it is almost not spicy, it may be rather spicy. So when you try some Mexican food, it will be a good idea to have a cup of milk. Remember, that water does not help when you suffer from spicy food.

9. DINNER AND A VIEW

If you like beautiful city views and delicious food, this place will be perfect for you. Crowne Plaza, located in Zona Diamante (part of Queretato), is not only a great hotel. This place has more to offer, it has a restaurant with a spectacular view of the city. People like to come here to celebrate there special occasions, enjoy the view and perfect service.

Obviously, the best time to come here will be in the evening. If you are planning to visit this restaurant on the weekend, do not forget about the reservation. In this way you can also choose a table with better view.

\>TOURIST

10. BEST MARGARITA

Mexico is well known for its tequila which is necessary for a margarita. There is one place in Queretatro where you can get just a perfect one. When you are in downtown visit San Miguelito. This is a Mexican restaurant that will surprise you in many ways. First of all, they serve margaritas of many different flavours: strawberry, peach, pomegranet, coconut, lime etc. This place has many bright and lovely decorations that resemble Mexican style and culture and their stuff speaks good English.

As we started talking about margaritas, let me warn you. In some restaurants they have a promotion two for one margaritas. When you order them, they may offer you variety of different tequilas. Ask for they one they use for promotion, otherwise they will charge you more.

11. CHEESE AND WINE ROUTES

Just outside Queretaro there are several vineyards. There you can see how grape grows, the process of wine making etc. You can taste and buy wine here, they also sell different types of cheese for you to enjoy with your wine. In many vineyards it is possible to spend time there drinkig and taking pleasure from lovely Mexican weather. In some vineyards they have very little shade. Thus, if you want to spend some time there take your sunscreen and a hat.

12. PEÑA DE BERNAL

This beautiful place is also called Bernal's Boulder or Bernal Peak. Some people call it a mountain, which is wrong, it is a 433 m (1,421 ft) tall monolith. Many visitors perform a pilgrimage to the small chapel located at the highest point accessible through hiking. If you decide to do that, dress up in layers and avoid wearing dark clothes.

Once you are here go visit the town located near the monolit. They have a square where you can take wonderful pictures with Peña de Bernal. Also take some time for walking down the streets or in the downtown of this madgical place. It will be unforgettable.

13. PIRAMID

There are many things Mexico is famous for, one of them is piramids. Luckily we have one in Queretaro. The place is called El Cerrito Archeological Zone, also known as El Pueblito Piramid (not without a reason). It is located in the part of the city called El Pueblito.

This was a place of worshipe for local cultures, their town was built in front of the pyramid. Unfortunatelly, with the arrival of Spaniards their time was over. Nowadays we can see the evidence of colonists' presence – they built a house on top of the pyramid.

Visiting the piramid is free of charge and they also have a guide to tell you the history of this place. On weekdays it is open from 9 am till 4 pm and on weekends from 9 am till 7 pm. When you go there, don't forget to take sunblock as in some places there is not enough shade.

14. EL MIRADOR

El Mirador is a Spanish word for a viewpoint. Spectacular view opens from this point, you can see the city and its symbol – los arcos. This is a place where you should go to take beautiful pictures, spend time with your significant other and see the sunset.

It is located near a church called Templo de la Cruz, and a little market on the square in front of the church. Mostly what they sell there are souvenirs.

15. LOS ARCOS

Los Arcos is a symbol of the city. This is a 1,280 m long construction that consists of 74 arches. They were built in 18th century to supply Queretaro with water, however, there are many legends about the initial reason of their construction. Los Arcos definitely should be on your list of sightseeing as it is a magnificent historical monument.

Good thing about Los Arcos part of the city is that you can find plenty of different restaurants and bars there.

16. TEQUISQUIAPAN

You may be wondering what this almost impossible to pronounce word means. Well, this is the name of a town that is located 40 minutes away from Queretaro. There are several reasons to visit it. First of all the downtown area is fantastic, it has relaxing

>TOURIST

atmosphere and incredible arcitecture, its church is several centuries old. All this is a legacy of colonial time.

Tequisquiapan is a part of Queretaro's Ruta de Vino y Queso, so on your way there or back you can visit La Redonda (vine producer) or Bocanegra Cava de Quesos and try some cheese there. Another thing you should know about this town is that it has a market where you can buy some souvenirs that won't be expensive. There they also sell clothes, accessories and house decoration.

17. PARQUE BICENTENARIO

If you want to spend an enjoyable day with your family, this is the best place to go. The park has an entrance fee of 50 pesos, but all the rides are free. Security guards will noy allow you to enter with food and water, they ask to leave it at the gates.

There are activities for everybody – rides for all ages, small animal farm, waterpark, zip-line, planty of food outlets, picnic zone, beautiful gardens and paths to stroll. To certain extent it is a theme park. They have a huge dinosaur stature at the entrance and some dinosaur rides for kids. If you decide to go there, better do this in the morning, it will not be too hot.

18. CITY MYTHS

If you like legends and mystery, you will enjoy this tour. When in downtown you will see people dressed up in 18th century clothes. They offer a tour around the city center, which takes less than 2 hours. Professional actors will tell you legends about the city.

You will be taken to several locations, all within walking distance from one another. At each spot there are actors to perfrom for you, sometimes they jump out to surprise the visitors. Actors speek Spanish, but don't worry if your Spanish is not that good, you will still enjoy the performance and mysterious atmosphere. The price may vary, it will approximately cost you 200 pesos.

19. ALL THE BARS

In the downtown there is a street called 5 de Mayo. The street is very well known in Queretaro because it is full of restaurants and bars. There are plany of them: cuban, irish, british… you have a great variety to choose from. If you go there, you should take several things into consideration. First of all, if it is weekend, make a reservation, everything will be packed. Same thing will happen if it is quincena (day when Mexicans are paid, it is every 15th and 31st day of the month). If you go by car, think ahead, because most likely there will be no parking space and you will end up parking somewhere far. To avoid this better take an uber.

If you are looking for a bar with live music you can go to Hanks, which is not too far from 5 de Mayo. Another option is King Buffalo on Constituentes, 10 minutes from the downtown by car. They have a band every Wedneday and Friday night.

20. GRACIAS A DIOS

«Thanks to God» - this is the translation of this bar's name. which is also a pun. If you say the name fast in Spanish, it will sound like «thanks, goodbye». The bar is located in the downtown, people love it for its cool funky vibe and a great selection of mezcal. The bar also serves cocktails, beer and simple food which is delicious and reasonably priced. Part of the bar is indoors, the other has an open roof. If you want to go there at night, be sure to make a reservation, normally it is full at this time.

21. DOWNTOWN OASIS

Jardin Zinea is a beautiful garden in the heart of the city. This place is calm during the day, but becomes rather lively in the evening. There are street performers, people dancing salsa, orchestra playing, lots of food vendors. You can recognize the garden by its remarkable kiosk, where you can sit in peace. The garden is surrounded by nice stores and restaurants, it provides a shady refuge on a hot day. You definitely should not miss this place. However, when you come there on weekend afternoon, don't be surprised, because there will be many families enjoying their time.

22. FAIRS

Fairs are often organised on weekends and take place in one of the city's squares, that are all withing walking distance. Fairs are different - sometimes there are mostly vendors of traditional Mexican food, sometimes it is a book fair. Books they sell are rather cheap, for example one of Franz Kafka's book costed me 20 pesos. You can find there books both in English and Spanish.

>TOURIST

23. FOREIGNERS' PARADE

Every March communities of foreigners together with Queretaro's government organise a parade to share the culture with citizens. This is an amzing event because people from more than 70 countires participate in the parade, they wear traditional costumes, hold there flags and walk from the downtown to los Arcos. This event is entertaining, educational and commpletely free of charge. You can take pictures, meet people from your country who live in Mexico now, and make new friends. This event starts in the afternoon, so it is not too hot, and lasts for a little more than an hour and a half.

24. FOREIGNERS' FESTIVAL

In Spanish it is called Festival Extranjeros and it takes place in the mid April and lasts for several days. Footbal stadium is its venue. This place was chosen because thousands of people come there to enjoy other cultures. Every country has its own stand decorated according to their national style, they sell traditional homemade food, alcohol, souvenires and other specialties from their countries.

There are people from all over the world – from North and South America, Europe, Africa, Asia…you will need more than one day to see everything that this festival offers. There are some favorites among countries – those are the stands of Italy, the Netherlands, Austria, Germany, Scotland, Ireland, Lebanon, Japan and Turkey. People are very interested in them for a simple reason, they sell good beer or other alcohol and delicious food. There is an entrance fee, but it is not expensive at all and totally worth it.

Also note that it is extremely popular event in the city and most likely it is held on weekend, so it will be rather crowded in the afternoon. In addition to that you need to make sure you take enough money. Believe me, even if you don't plan to spend much, you will. And I will tell you there is nothing bad, in some cases it will be one time opportunity to try Kazakhstan honey beer or real sake or German pretzel made by a German using his grandma's recipe, buy a pair of shorts with a funny print from South Africa, an amber bracelet from Lithuenia. You will dance like crazy with dutch people and their dj sets and sing the Beatles' songs with Brits, etc.

>TOURIST

The festival is not only about spending money. There is a stage where foreigners perform. They sing in their native language and dance traditional dances.

25. QUERETARO'S COMIC-CON

Conque is Queretaro's analogue of Comic-Con. It is held annualy in May and lasts for several days. They invite actors, producers, cartoonists, comic creators, etc. Organizers creat a programme for several days, that differs every year. If you want to visit Conque, it will be a good idea to buy your tickets in advance. And just a fair warning, those tickets will not be the cheapest, but still affordable.

26. MUSEO REGIONAL

You may not be a museum fan, but this one is worth visiting. Museo Regional is the place where you can learn so much about Mexican history and culture. It takes you through the time – first you see what life of a native indian was like, prehispanic times, colonial times, revolution, fight for independence, and post-revolution time.

Displays are well organised with clear route, so you will always understand the seequence of events.

The museum is rather big and occupies 2 floors. You will enjoy walking there, as the building itself is an exquisite piece of architecture that worth your attention. Museums courtyard is majestic! You can take pictures there with fontains and beautiful museum on the background. As in many museums there is an entrance fee. In Museo Regional it is 60 pesos.

27. HANDICRAFT FAIRS AND STORES

If you are looking for unusual souvenires, accessories, homemade sweets or alcohol made by an author's recipe or some new decorations for your house, then this is th place to go. Handicraft fairs are organised rather often, mostly in the downtown area. There you can find vendors of handmade jewelary, mezcal with different tastes (coffee, strawberry, pineapple), handmade toys, leather products, etc.

Apart from fairs you can also check some stores. For instance, Quinto Real on 5 de Mayo Street is a shop with adorable gifts and souvenirs from all over the country, other little things, organic lotions and beauty products. On Francisco I. Madero Street, you can find a store called Madre Tierra. There they also sell many cute and interesting things for gifts, natural tea and organic soap.

28. DOLLS

When you are walking in the downtown, you will see old ladies selling handmade rag dolls. These dolls have become a symbol of Queretaro and they can be of any size. They are called Marias and they have been made in Mexico since colonial times. Now they are popular all over the country, but the experts say they originate in the state of Queretaro.

You can aslo see them in souvenirs shops, but it will definitely be cheaper to buy them from street vendors, there is no difference in dolls they sell in the stores and on the streets. If you buy them on the streets, you will support old Mexican ladies who make them. This dolls are their source of income.

Apart from the dolls they can also sell wooden donkeys and clay piggy banks. They are rather cute, but for some reason they have not become as popular as the dolls.

29. DIA DE LOS MUERTOS

If you are thinking about comming to Queretaro in Autumn, better choose end of October/ beginning of November. First of all, by that time rainy season will be over and it will not be too hot. Secondly, there will be a very important event.

Also known as Day of the Dead it is selebrated in November in connection with the Catholic holidaya of All Saints' Day (November 1) and All Souls' Day (November 2). There are many traditions connected with this day: people build altars to honour their dead members of family, sugar skulls are sold everywhere and, of course, there is a festival.

People paint there faces, dress up like Catrina (Mexican Lady of Death), there are many events going on in the downtown. For example, three squares in the downtown offer different things – food stalls, flower alters, performances, city legends tour, etc. You will see many flowers for sale. They are marigold flowers, known in Mexico as flowers of the deads and they are the key element of the celebration. There are some events in other parts of the city aslo, but the majority of them take place in the city center.

>TOURIST

30. MEXICAN INDEPENDENCE DAY CELEBRATION

On the 16th of September Mexico celebrates its independence from Spain. This is the day for tourists to feel the culture and to share the joy with Mexicans. It is an official day off, so you will see many people outside, you will hear them shouting «animo!».

Many events will take place downtown, there will be people in colourful outfits, performers, flags, green, white and red colours everywhere, music and fireworks at night. If you are thinking about comming to Queretaro in September, make sure you will not miss this special celebration.

31. SILENT PROCESSION

Silent Procession originates in Spain and when Spainyards came to Mexico, they brought it together with many other traditions, that have rooted deeply in Mexican culture. The procession takes place on Good Friday, in the evening. Men, women and children covered in robe from head to toes, walk barefoot. Some of them beat themselves in public, some are chained, some hold crosses.

This event may not be for everybody, to some people it can even be rather scary. However, this is part of Mexican traditions, it can be a truly solemn experience, that you will never forget because of how impressive it is. You will hardly hear people's steps and there dedication and believe will make everybody think for a while.

32. HOLIDAYS ARE FOR EVERYONE

Of course holidays are for everyone, but what I mean is that when we are having fun many people still have to work. So what happens in Queretaro is that during Christmas days and Easter many restaurants and shops are closed, so do not be surprised.

However, big supermarkets, some banks and cinemas will be open. In addition to this many people will leave Queretaro to spend holidays with families in their home towns.

33. MOVIES

If you feel spontaneous desire to go to the movies, go there without hesitating. Don't be afraid that everything is in Spanish, they also show movies in English. There are 2 chains of cinemas in Queretaro – they are Cinepolis and Cinemex. Cinepolis is a little bit more expensive, but seats are much more comfortable. Cinemas are located in the malls, luckily, they are all around the city.

You also don't have to rush: let's say movie you want to watch starts at 7 pm, but it's 7:15. Buy a ticket, commercials last for half an hour, I am not exaggerating.

34. SIERRA GORDA

Sierra Gorda is a Biosphere Reserve in Queretaro state. Hikes, explorers, and nature admirers will enjoy this extremely beautiful place rugged with steep mountains and deep canyons. Fantastic thing about this reserve is that it is located in several different climate zones. When you are there, you will feel the climate change from semi-desert to rainforest.

Sierra Gorda has many amazing things to offer: churches and chapels protected by the UNESCO, majestic nature, waterfalls, foggy mountains, gardens, valleys, some special places like Heaven's gates.

There are many tours you can book and they include transportation, guide, accommodation and meals. When we are talking about accomodation there, don't expect a luxury hotel. In most cases it will be a little pretty hotel close to nature with kind owners that will meet you.

Remember that during certain dates (Independence Week, Christmas, Easter Week), there will be many people and it also will be quite challanging to find accomodation. To really explore Sierra Gorda you will need at least 4 days, but there are tours for more and less days.

35. ESCONDIDO PLACE

Beautiful natural park in the state of Queretaro, an hour away from the city of Queretaro. The park is perfect for family getaway as it is very spacious, it has 2 lakes, 7 pools, termal waters, saunas and lots of vegetation.

One of the greatest things about Escondido is that you can make BBQs there. This is very beautiful and popular place, so if you are planning to go there on weekends, better arrive early. It has entrance fee of 150 pesos. They will let you in with your food, but alcohol is not allowed. However, they give you an option to buy it in the park.

Summer will not be the best time to go there due to the rainy season. Most days in summer are cloudy and it rains quite often.

36. GOLF IN QUERETARO

Good news for golfers – there are several golf courses in Queretaro. There are 9 and 18 holes courses; they all have different promotions and prices vary. Also location can be different – within the city or on the outskirts, like Zibata Golf, which is considered to be a pristige golf course. It lies on the hills and has a great view of the city.

37. WEEKEND REST FOR EVERYBODY

The situation is almost the same as with the holidays – business is closed on Sunday. You can think it is prety obvious, but situation in Mexico may be a little different. Things you don't expect to be closed may be closed. It means, that many shops, except for malls and supermarkets, markets will be closed. Restaurants are open, but close earlier than usually. On Saturday many establishments also close much earlier. So, please, don't forget about this Mexican tendency when you are planning something.

38. PUBLIC TRANSPORT IN QUERETARO

The city is rather big and it is constantly growing, but despite this fact, we don't have any variety in public transport, it is only represented by busses. The system of public transportation is, unfortunately, far from being perfect. For example, there are so many buses that have the same route and they all go one after another. This is one of the reasons we have to make several transfers when we go somewhere.

Another problem is in payment. In some buses you pay with cash, in some you need to pay with a special card that you need to buy beforehand, but the problem is that they don't sell them on every bus stop.

All in all, traveling by bus in Queretaro is not easy, but not impossible. If you ask me, as a tourist I would rather go by Uber than by bus.

39. UBER VS TAXI IN QUERETARO

Taxi drivers dislike Uber drivers a lot and sometimes they even have conflicts. This is one of the reasons Uber drivers never stay very close to the malls, restaurants, cinemas, etc. They avoid taxi drivers who park there.

If we are talking about the price, Uber is cheaper, but not significantly. Tipping Uber drivers is unncommon in Mexico and probably they would be very surprised if you tip. With some of the taxi drivers it is possible to negotiate the price, but don't count on it, many of them are rather stingy. At the taxi stands, while waiting for customers, they would rather push the cars than drive. Especially often you can see this at the bus stations. Personally I would prefer Uber, because their cars are more comfortable and the drivers are more likely to speak English.

40. RENTAL CAR

Having your own car and going anywhere anytime is great, but if you decid to have a rental can in Queretaro, you should remember about several things. Mexican people tend to speed and some of them are reckless drivers. The reason for this behaviour is unknown, but Mexicans themselves admit that they can be crazy on the road.

Another problem that a car owner will face is parking, especially in downtown. Even though we have public garages it is not enough. Parking on the street is not a solution as street are narrow and in some parts of the town it is forbidden to park on the street. Tricky thing about downtown is that they don't really have no parking signs everywhere, so you may find a perfect place, park there and when you return you will notice a ticket. The reason for this was explained to me. The government does not want to disfigure downtown with signs, but the police expects you to figure out that you are not supposed to park in some places even without a sign.

41. GREETINGS

There is an old tradition in Mexico to give a kiss on the cheeck as a greeting. Although, now some people start to shake hands instead of kissing. So we can say that it depends on a person. Still more people prefer to give a kiss and fewer to shake hands. If you see that somebody is going to give you a kiss, don't be surprised and don't retreat, as this may be offensive. Mexicans are very touchy-feely people and this explains a lot in their behaviour.

42. FOREIGNERS

As a foreigner I noticed that there are 3 categories of people with different attitudes. First goup of people loves you. They will ask you millions of questions about your country, introduce you to their family and friends, buy you a drink and give planty of tips about where to go and what to do. Most likely they will be the ones to start the conversation and they will definitely ask whether you like Mexico and what you think about spicy food. Another group of people do not really like foreigners, so they will just pay very little attention to you and mind there business. Last group of people just want to practice their English, so if they hear you speaking this language, they will probably make a nice small talk and that is it.

It does not matter with what category of people you have to deal, if you ask them for help, they will never say no. You don't need to be shy to ask any question, Mexican people are very helpful.

43. GRINGOS

This word is used for people from the USA. Nowadays this term is becoming less and less offensive. Mexicans also tend to use this word referring to other foreigners. For some reason if you speak English, they automatically assume that you are from the USA.

In most cases, when a Mexican uses the word «gringo» reffering to you, this is not an offence, he is just joking. Mexicans like jokes and fun, they give each other nicknames, but not to offend. For example, they can call plump people «pansa» which means a belly.

44. COMMUNICATION

In Mexico many people still don't speak English. Even the fact that this country borders with the USA does not help. In many restaurants, private hospitals and malls workers speak English, from time to time you can see an English speaking person on the street, there are also many tours with English speaking guides, but to feel comfortable in Mexico I would recommend you to learn some basics of Spanish before you come.

45. IF YOU NEED HELP WITH SPANISH

In case your knowledge of Spanish is not that great, but you need some documentation to be done or you need to understand what people say, you can go to language schools. They don't only offer language classes, they also have professional translators and interpreters to help you. There are plenty of such schools, mostly they are located closer to the downtown area – Constituentes Avenue, Francisco I. Madero Street, Tecnologico Avenue. Prices for the services vary, but you should remember that they will not be cheap.

46. IF YOU DON'T FEEL WELL

Nobody wants to get sick during vacation, but it may happen unexpectedly. If you find yourself in a situation like that, you don't have to worry. Here you have several options: if you are sure it is not something serous, maybe a cold, you can go to the pharmacy and a doctor will attend you there. Framacias del Ahorro and Farmacias Similares provide medical service, consultation there will cost around 50 pesos. On the other hand, if you feel that you have more serious problem, you definitely should go to the hospital. In all private hospitals there are doctors who speak English. Also, good thing is that there are hospitals in every part of the city. Please not, that a consultation in private hospital may be more than 500 pesos.

There are also public hospitals which are called IMMS. If I were you, I would not even try going there. People need to wait more than 3 hours to be attended and doctors are indifferent. On top of that you need to have special documents to be attended there.

47. THINGS YOU SHOULD NOT FORGET

When you are packing make sure you take at least one jacket if you are visiting Queretaro during the raining season. Also during this time you would want to have an umbrella and a pair of shoes that do not get wet (I am not talking about Wellington boots, these will be too much).

Another thing is pretty obvious, but we very often forget about it. Food in Mexico is very different and when people come here they sometimes face such problems as diarhea or constipation. To avoid these problems, make sure you take some medicine for stomach with you. If you are already in Queretaro and you are having these problems, go to the pharmacy and ask for Treda or Nifuroxazida.

48. PEOPLE ASKING FOR MONEY

One of the Mexican problems is poverty, elderly people, adults and children are impacted by it. You will see people of different ages asking for money on the streets, they may be selling some little things like chocolates, flowers, souvenirs, toys. Remember, that if somebody asks you for money on the street, you do not have to pay, it is only you decision.

If you decide to give some money, think twice about it, in many cases people come up with touchy stories, but it is not true, children can be at school, but they or their parents choose asking for money over it. Mexico is a poor country, but you can find a job here and these people just chose not to. So, please, remember that in many cases it is not charity, you simply help people earn money.

49. EXPLORE NEIGHBOURING STATES

Queretaro state is located in the middle of the country and borders with Guanajuato, Hidalgo, Morelia, and State of Mexico. If you have a lot of time here in Queretaro, I would also recommend you take a day trip to one of this states.

Depending on the time of the year, there are many different event in the neighbouring states. For example in winter you can visit monarch butterfly's sanctuaries in Morelia. They are fantastic places. First of all, you will see thousands of butterflies flying around, second of all, you will be amazed by the nature. Normally you need go hike a hill in the forest to see all the butterflies. So once you are there, you will see valley, mountains, forest and butterflies, of course. City Guanajuato in the state of Guanojuato also worth visiting. The city is located on hills and has an astonishing architecture and views. There are lots of museums, mummies and other places to visit. In december they organise a music faestival. So once you are in Queretaro, don't miss fantastic experience you may get only several hours away from the city.

>TOURIST

50. BEST PLACES TO TAKE PICTURES

Vacation is wonderful time and pictures help us to keep memories about it forever. Of course everybody wants to have outstanding pictures. I will tell you about some places where you can get such pictures in Queretaro.

Queretaro is old and beautiful city, so your pictures will be nice pretty much anywhere you take them. However, if you want exquisite pictures you should go to Pueblo Magico, Peña de Bernal (there is Plaza San Sebastian Bernal where you can take a picture with the monolit and beautiful buildings), courtyard of Museo de Arte de Queretaro, narrow streets of Centro Historico in the downtown, inside of the Templo de Santa Rosa de Vitebro, everywhere in Sierra Gorda, El Cerrito (they have lots of vegetation and the piramid).

>TOURIST

TOP REASONS TO BOOK THIS TRIP

Queretaro is the safest city in Mexico, it is located in the middle of the country, close to other significant states. This is perfect place to experience Mexico.

In Queretaro we have plenty of things to do! You can say thre same about every city in Mexico. There are so many things you can explore both inside and outside the city. Historical sights, vivid nightlife, art, places to have fun with the whole family – this city has things to offer to people of different interests.

Many festivals are organised in Queretaro. They may be wine festivals, cultural festivals, music festivals, etc. It does not matter when you come, there will be a festival for you to participate in. Expositions also regularily take place here.

Diversity of food will amaze you. We have a great deal of street sellers of Mexican food, many Mexican restaurants, European and Lebanon cuisine, wings restaurants… You will have a great choice when you come here.

Queretaro is also known for nice people. They like to say hello when they see you on the street, they are always polite, very helpful, never aggressive and do not forget to say «thank you».

\>TOURIST

BONUS BOOK

50 THINGS TO KNOW ABOUT PACKING LIGHT FOR TRAVEL

PACK THE RIGHT WAY EVERY TIME

AUTHOR: MANIDIPA BHATTACHARYYA

First Published in 2015 by Dr. Lisa Rusczyk. Copyright 2015. All Rights Reserved. No part of this publication may be reproduced, including scanning and photocopying, or distributed in any form or by any means, electronic or mechanical, or stored in a database or retrieval system without prior written permission from the publisher.

Disclaimer: The publisher has put forth an effort in preparing and arranging this book. The information provided herein by the author is provided "as is". Use this information at your own risk. The publisher is not a licensed doctor. Consult your doctor before engaging in any medical activities. The publisher and author disclaim any liabilities for any loss of profit or commercial or personal damages resulting from the information contained in this book.

Edited by Melanie Howthorne

ABOUT THE AUTHOR

Manidipa Bhattacharyya is a creative writer and editor, with an education in English literature and Linguistics. After working in the IT industry for seven long years she decided to call it quits and follow her heart instead. Manidipa has been ghost writing, editing, proof reading and doing secondary research services for many story tellers and article writers for about three years. She stays in Kolkata, India with her husband and a busy two year old. In her own time Manidipa enjoys travelling, photography and writing flash fiction.

Manidipa believes in travelling light and never carries anything that she couldn't haul herself on a trip. However, travelling with her child changed the scenario. She seemed to carry the entire world with her for the baby on the first two trips. But good sense prevailed and she is again working her way to becoming a light traveler, this time with a kid.

INTRODUCTION

*He who would travel happily
must travel light.*

-Antoine de Saint-Exupéry

Travel takes you to different places from seas and mountains to deserts and much more. In your travels you get to interact with different people and their cultures. You will, however, enjoy the sights and interact positively with these new people even more, if you are travelling light.

When you travel light your mind can be free from worry about your belongings. You do not have to spend precious vacation time waiting for your luggage to arrive after a long flight. There is be no chance of your bags going missing and the best part is that you need not pay a fee for checked baggage.

People who have mastered this art of packing light will root for you to take only one carry-on, wherever you go. However, many people can find it really hard to pack light. More so if you are travelling with children. Differentiating between "must have" and "just in case" items is the starting point. There will be ample shopping avenues at your destination which are just waiting to be explored.

This book will show you 'packing' in a new 'light' – pun intended – and help you to embrace light packing practices for all of your future travels.

Off to packing!

DEDICATION

I dedicate this book to all the travel buffs that I know, who have given me great insights into the contents of their backpacks.

THE RIGHT TRAVEL GEAR

1. CHOOSE YOUR TRAVEL GEAR CAREFULLY

While selecting your travel gear, pick items that are light weight, durable and most importantly, easy to carry. There are cases with wheels so you can drag them along – these are usually on the heavy side because of the trolley. Alternatively a backpack that you can carry comfortably on your back, or even a duffel bag that you can carry easily by hand or sling across your body are also great options. Whatever you choose, one thing to keep in mind is that the luggage itself should not weigh a ton, this will give you the flexibility to bring along one extra pair of shoes if you so desire.

>TOURIST

2. CARRY THE MINIMUM NUMBER OF BAGS

Selecting light weight luggage is not everything. You need to restrict the number of bags you carry as well. One carry-on size bag is ideal for light travel. Most carriers allow one cabin baggage plus one purse, handbag or camera bag as long as it slides under the seat in front. So technically, you can carry two items of luggage without checking them in.

3. PACK ONE EXTRA BAG

Always pack one extra empty bag along with your essential items. This could be a very light weight duffel bag or even a sturdy tote bag which takes up minimal space. In the event that you end up buying a lot of souvenirs, you already have a handy bag to stuff all that into and do not have to spend time hunting for an appropriate bag.

I'm very strict with my packing and have everything in its right place. I never change a rule. I hardly use anything in the hotel room. I wheel my own wardrobe in and that's it.

Charlie Watts

CLOTHES & ACCESSORIES

4. PLAN AHEAD

Figure out in advance what you plan to do on your trip. That will help you to pick that one dress you need for the occasion. If you are going to attend a wedding then you have to carry formal wear. If not, you can ditch the gown for something lighter that will be comfortable during long walks or on the beach.

5. WEAR THAT JACKET

Remember that wearing items will not add extra luggage for your air travel. So wear that bulky jacket that you plan to carry for your trip. This saves space and can also help keep you warm during the chilly flight.

6. MIX AND MATCH

Carry clothes that can be interchangeably used to reinvent your look. Find one top that goes well with a couple of pairs of pants or skirts. Use tops, shirts and jackets wisely along with other accessories like a scarf or a stole to create a new look.

7. CHOOSE YOUR FABRIC WISELY

Stuffing clothes in cramped bags definitely takes its toll which results in wrinkles. It is best to carry wrinkle free, synthetic clothes or merino tops. This will eliminate the need for that small iron you usually bring along.

8. DITCH CLOTHES PACK UNDERWEAR

Pack more underwear and socks. These are the things that will give you a fresh feel even if you do not get a chance to wear fresh clothes. Moreover these are easy to wash and can be dried inside the hotel room itself.

9. CHOOSE DARK OVER LIGHT

While picking your clothes choose dark coloured ones. They are easy to colour coordinate and can last longer before needing a wash. Accidental food spills and dirt from the road are less visible on darker clothes.

10. WEAR YOUR JEANS

Take only one pair of Jeans with you, which you should wear on the flight. Remember to pick a pair that can be worn for sightseeing trips and is equally eloquent for dinner. You can add variety by adding light weight cargoes and chinos.

11. CARRY SMART ACCESSORIES

The right accessory can give you a fresh look even with the same old dress. An intelligent neck-piece, a couple of bright scarves, stoles or a sarong can be used in a number of ways to add variety to your clothing. These light weight beauties can double up as a nursing cover, a light blanket, beach wear, a modesty cover for visiting places of worship, and also makes for an enthralling game of peek-a-boo.

12. LEARN TO FOLD YOUR GARMENTS

Seasoned travellers all swear by rolling their clothes for compact and wrinkle free packing. Bundle packing, where you roll the clothes around a central object as if tying it up, is also a popular method of compact and wrinkle free packing. Stacking folded clothes one on top of another is a big no-no as it makes creases extreme and they are difficult to get rid of without ironing.

13. WASH YOUR DIRTY LAUNDRY

One of the ways to avoid carrying loads of clothes is to wash the clothes you carry. At some places you might get to use the laundry services or a Laundromat but if you are in a pinch, best solution is to wash them yourself. If that is the plan then carrying quick drying clothes is highly recommended, which most often also happen to be the wrinkle free variety.

14. LEAVE THOSE TOWELS BEHIND

Regular towels take up a lot of space, are heavy and take ages to dry out. If you are staying at hotels they will provide you with towels anyway. If you are travelling to a remote place, where the availability of towels look doubtful, carry a light weight travel towel of viscose material to do the job.

15. USE A COMPRESSION BAG

Compression bags are getting lots of recommendation now days from regular travellers. These are useful for saving space in your luggage when you have to pack bulky dresses. While packing for the return trip, get help from the hotel staff to arrange a vacuum cleaner.

FOOTWEAR

16. PUT ON YOUR HIKING BOOTS

If you have plans to go hiking or trekking during your trip, you will need those bulky hiking boots. The best way to carry them is to wear them on flight to save space and luggage weight. You can remove the boots once inside and be comfortable in your socks.

17. PICKING THE RIGHT SHOES

Shoes are often the bulkiest items, along with being the dainty if you are a female. They need care and take up a lot of space in your luggage. It is advisable therefore to pick shoes very carefully. If you plan to do a lot of walking and site seeing, then wearing a pair of comfortable walking shoes are a must. For more formal occasions you can carry durable, light weight flats which will not take up much space.

18. STUFF SHOES

If you happen to pack a pair of shoes, ensure you utilize their hollow insides. Tuck small items like rolled up socks or belts to save space. They will also be easy to find.

>TOURIST

TOILETRIES

19. STASHING TOILETRIES

Carry only absolute necessities. Airline rules dictate that for one carry-on bag, liquids and gels must be in 3.4 ounce (100ml) bottles or less, and must be packed in a one quart zip-lock bag. If you are planning to stay in a hotel, the basic things will be provided for you. It's best is to buy the rest from the local market at your destination.

20. TAKE ALONG TAMPONS

Tampons are a hard to find item in a lot of countries. Figure out how many you need and pack accordingly. For longer stays you can buy them online and have them delivered to where you are staying.

21. GET PAMPERED BEFORE YOU TRAVEL

Some avid travellers suggest getting a pedicure and manicure just the day before travelling. This not only gives you a well kept look, you also save the trouble of packing nail polish. Remember, every little bit of weight reduced adds up.

ELECTRONICS
22. LUGGING ALONG ELECTRONICS

Electronics have a large role to play in our lives today. Most of us cannot imagine our lives away from our phones, laptops or tablets. However while travelling, one must consider the amount of weight these electronics add to our luggage. Thankfully smart phones come along with all the essentials tools like a camera, email access, picture editing tools and more. They are smart to the point of eliminating the need to carry multiple gadgets. Choose a smart phone that suits all your requirements and travel with the world in your palms or pocket.

23. REDUCE THE NUMBER OF CHARGERS

If you do travel with multiple electronic devices, you will have to bear the additional burden of carrying all their chargers too. Check if a single charger can be used for multiple devices. You might also consider investing in a pocket charger. These small devices support multiple devices while keeping you charged on the go.

\>TOURIST

24. TRAVEL FRIENDLY APPS

Along with smart phones come numerous apps, which are immensely helpful in our travels. You name it and you have an app for it at hand – take pictures, sharing with friends and family, torch to light dark roads, maps, checking flight/train times, find hotels and many other things. Use these smart alternatives to traditional items like books to eliminate weight and save space.

> *I get ideas about what's essential when packing my suitcase.*

-Diane von Furstenberg

TRAVELLING WITH KIDS

25. BRING ALONG THE STROLLER

Kids might enjoy walking for a while but they soon tire out and a stroller is the just the right thing for them to rest in while you continue your tour. Strollers also double duty as a luggage carrier and shopping bag holder. Remember to pick a light weight, easy to handle brand of stroller. Better yet, find out in advance if you can rent a stroller at your destination.

26. BRING ONLY ENOUGH DIAPERS FOR YOUR TRIP

Diapers take up a lot of space and add to the weight of your luggage. Therefore it is advisable to carry just enough diapers to last through the trip and a few for afterwards, till you buy fresh stock at your destination. Unless of course you are travelling to a really remote area, in which case you have no choice but to carry the load. Otherwise diapers are something you will find pretty easily.

27. TAKE ONLY A COUPLE OF TOYS

Children are easily attracted by new things in their environment. While travelling they will find numerous 'new' objects to scrutinize and play with. Packing just one favorite toy is enough, or if there is no favorite toy leave out all of them in favor of stories or imaginary games.

28. CARRY KID FRIENDLY SNACKS

Create a small snack counter in your bag to store away quick bites for those sudden hunger pangs. Depending on the child's age this could include chocolates, raisins, dry fruits, granola bars or biscuits. Also keep a bottle of water handy for your little one. These things do not add much weight and can be adjusted in a handbag or knapsack.

29. GAMES TO CARRY

Create some travel specific, imaginary games if you have slightly grown up children, like spot the attractions. Keep a coloring book and colors handy for in-flight or hotel time. Apps on your smart phone can keep the children engaged with cartoons and story books. Older children are often entertained by games available on phones or tablets. This cuts the weight of luggage down while keeping the kids entertained.

30. LET THE KIDS CARRY THEIR LOAD

A good thing is to start early sharing of responsibilities. Let your child pick a bag of his or her choice and pack it themselves. Keep tabs on what they are stuffing in their bags by asking if they will be using that item on the trip. It could start out being just an entertainment bag initially but with growing years they will learn to sort the useful from the superfluous. Children as little as four can maneuver a small trolley suitcase like a pro- their experience in pull along toys credit. If you are worried that you may be pulling it for them, you may want to start with a backpack.

31. DECIDE ON LOCATION FOR CHILDREN TO SLEEP

While on a trip you might not always get a crib at your destination, and carrying one will make life all the more difficult. Instead call ahead to see if there are any cribs or roll out beds for children. You may even put blankets on the floor. Weave them a story about camping and they will gladly sleep without any trouble.

32. GET BABY PRODUCTS DELIVERED AT YOUR DESTINATION

If you are absolutely paranoid about not getting your favourite variety of diaper or brand of baby food, check out online stores like amazon.com for services in your destination city. You can buy things online ahead of your travel and get them delivered to your hotel upon arrival.

33. FEEDING NEEDS OF YOUR INFANTS

If you are travelling with a breastfed infant, you save the trouble of carrying bottles and bottle sanitization kits. For special food, or medications, you may need to call ahead to make sure you have a refrigerator where you are staying.

34. FEEDING NEEDS OF YOUR TODDLER

With the progression from infancy to toddler, their dietary requirements too evolve. You will have to pack some snacks for travelling time. Fresh fruits and vegetables can be purchased at your destination. Most of the cities you travel to in whichever part of the world, will have baby food products and formulas, available at the local drug-store or the supermarket.

35. PICKING CLOTHES FOR YOUR BABY

Contrary to popular belief, babies can do without many changes of clothes. At the most pack 2 outfits per day. Pack mix and match type clothes for your little one as well. Pick things which are comfortable to wear and quick to dry.

36. SELECTING SHOES FOR YOUR BABY

Like outfits, kids can make do with two pairs of comfortable shoes. If you can get some water resistant shoes it will be best. To expedite drying wet shoes, you can stuff newspaper in them then wrap them with newspaper and leave them to dry overnight.

37. KEEP ONE CHANGE OF CLOTHES HANDY

Travelling with kids can be tricky. Keep a change of clothes for the kids and mum handy in your purse or tote bag. This takes a bit of space in your hand luggage but comes extremely handy in case there are any accidents or spills.

38. LEAVE BEHIND BABY ACCESSORIES

Baby accessories like their bed, bath tub, car seat, crib etc. should be left at home. Many hotels provide a crib on request, while car seats can be borrowed from friends or rented. Babies can be given a bath in the hotel sink or even in the adult bath tub with a little bit of water. If you bring a few bath toys, they can be used in the bath, pool, and out of water. They can also be sanitized easily in the sink.

39. CARRY A SMALL LOAD OF PLASTIC BAGS

With children around there are chances of a number of soiled clothes and diapers. These plastic bags help to sort the dirt from the clean inside your big bag. These are very light weight and come in handy to other carry stuff as well at times.

PACK WITH A PURPOSE

40. PACKING FOR BUSINESS TRIPS

One neutral-colored suit should suffice. It can be paired with different shirts, ties and accessories for different occasions. One pair of black suit pants could be worn with a matching jacket for the office or with a snazzy top for dinner.

41. PACKING FOR A CRUISE

Most cruises have formal dinners, and that formal dress usually takes up a lot of space. However you might find a tuxedo to rent. For women, a short black dress with multiple accessory options will do the trick.

42. PACKING FOR A LONG TRIP OVER DIFFERENT CLIMATES

The secret packing mantra for travel over multiple climates is layering. Layering traps air around your body creating insulation against the cold. The same light t-shirt that is comfortable in a warmer climate can be the innermost layer in a colder climate.

REDUCE SOME MORE WEIGHT

43. LEAVE PRECIOUS THINGS AT HOME

Things that you would hate to lose or get damaged leave them at home. Precious jewelry, expensive gadgets or dresses, could be anything. You will not require these on your trip. Leave them at home and spare the load on your mind.

44. SEND SOUVENIRS BY MAIL

If you have spent all your money on purchasing souvenirs, carrying them back in the same bag that you brought along would be difficult. Either pack everything in another bag and check it in the airport or get everything shipped to your home. Use an international carrier for a secure transit, but this could be more expensive than the checking fees at the airport.

45. AVOID CARRYING BOOKS

Books equal to weight. There are many reading apps which you can download on your smart phone or tab. Plus there are gadgets like Kindle and Nook that are thinner and lighter alternatives to your regular book.

>TOURIST

CHECK, GET, SET, CHECK AGAIN

46. STRATEGIZE BEFORE PACKING

Create a travel list and prepare all that you think you need to carry along. Keep everything on your bed or floor before packing and then think through once again – do I really need that? Any item that meets this question can be avoided. Remove whatever you don't really need and pack the rest.

47. TEST YOUR LUGGAGE

Once you have fully packed for the trip take a test trip with your luggage. Take your bags and go to town for window shopping for an hour. If you enjoy your hour long trip it is good to go, if not, go home and reduce the load some more. Repeat this test till you hit the right weight.

48. ADD A ROLL OF DUCT TAPE

You might wonder why, when this book has been talking about reducing stuff, we're suddenly asking you to pack something totally unusual. This is because when you have limited supplies, duct tape is immensely helpful for small repairs – a broken bag, leaking zip-lock bag, broken sunglasses, you name it and duct tape can fix it, temporarily.

49. LIST OF ESSENTIAL ITEMS

Even though the emphasis is on packing light, there are things which have to be carried for any trip. Here is our list of essentials:

- Passport/Visa or any other ID

- Any other paper work that might be required on a trip like permits, hotel reservation confirmations etc.

- Medicines – all your prescription medicines and emergency kit, especially if you are travelling with children

- Medical or vaccination records

- Money in foreign currency if travelling to a different country

- Tickets- Email or Message them to your phone

50. MAKE THE MOST OF YOUR TRIP

Wherever you are going, whatever you hope to do we encourage you to embrace it whole-heartedly. Take in the scenery, the culture and above all, enjoy your time away from home.

>TOURIST

PACKING AND PLANNING TIPS

A Week before Leaving

- Arrange for someone to take care of pets and water plants
- Stop mail and newspaper
- Notify Credit Card companies where you are going.
- Change your thermostat settings
- Car inspected, oil is changed, and tires have the correct pressure.
- Passports and id is up to date.
- Pay bills.
- Copy important items and download travel Apps.
- Start collecting small bills for tips

Right Before Leaving

- Clean out refrigerator.
- Empty garbage cans.
- Lock windows.
- Make sure you have the right ID with you.
- Bring cash for tips.
- Remember travel documents.
- Lock door behind you.
- Remember wallet.
- Unplug items in house and pack chargers.

\>TOURIST

READ OTHER GREATER THAN A TOURIST BOOKS

Greater Than a Tourist San Miguel de Allende Guanajuato Mexico:
50 Travel Tips from a Local by Tom Peterson

Greater Than a Tourist – Lake George Area New York USA:
50 Travel Tips from a Local by Janine Hirschklau

Greater Than a Tourist – Monterey California United States:
50 Travel Tips from a Local by Katie Begley

Greater Than a Tourist – Chanai Crete Greece:
50 Travel Tips from a Local by Dimitra Papagrigoraki

Greater Than a Tourist – The Garden Route Western Cape Province South Africa:
50 Travel Tips from a Local by Li-Anne McGregor van Aardt

Greater Than a Tourist – Sevilla Andalusia Spain:
50 Travel Tips from a Local by Gabi Gazon

Greater Than a Tourist – Kota Bharu Kelantan Malaysia:
50 Travel Tips from a Local by Aditi Shukla

Children's Book: Charlie the Cavalier Travels the World by Lisa Rusczyk

> TOURIST

Visit Greater Than a Tourist for Free Travel Tips
http://GreaterThanATourist.com

Sign up for the Greater Than a Tourist Newsletter for discount days, new books, and travel information:
http://eepurl.com/cxspyf

Follow us on Facebook for tips, images, and ideas:
https://www.facebook.com/GreaterThanATourist

Follow us on Pinterest for travel tips and ideas:
http://pinterest.com/GreaterThanATourist

Follow us on Instagram for beautiful travel images:
http://Instagram.com/GreaterThanATourist

> TOURIST

Please leave your honest review of this book on Amazon and Goodreads. Please send your feedback to GreaterThanaTourist@gmail.com as we continue to improve the series. Thank you. We appreciate your positive and constructive feedback. Thank you.

> TOURIST

METRIC CONVERSIONS

TEMPERATURE

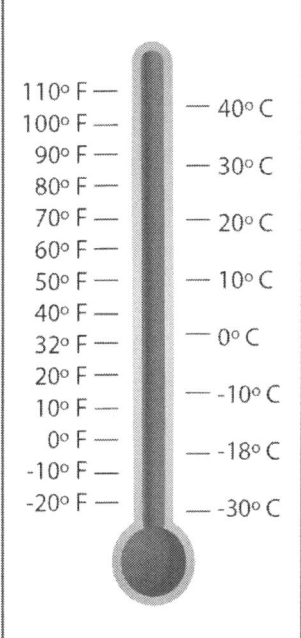

110° F — — 40° C
100° F —
90° F — — 30° C
80° F —
70° F — — 20° C
60° F —
50° F — — 10° C
40° F —
32° F — — 0° C
20° F —
10° F — — -10° C
0° F —
-10° F — — -18° C
-20° F — — -30° C

To convert F to C:

Subtract 32, and then multiply by 5/9 or .5555.

To Convert C to F:

Multiply by 1.8 and then add 32.

32F = 0C

LIQUID VOLUME

To Convert:................Multiply by
U.S. Gallons to Liters................ 3.8
U.S. Liters to Gallons 26
Imperial Gallons to U.S. Gallons 1.2
Imperial Gallons to Liters....... 4.55
Liters to Imperial Gallons 22
1 Liter = .26 U.S. Gallon
1 U.S. Gallon = 3.8 Liters

DISTANCE

To convert ....Multiply by
Inches to Centimeters 2.54
Centimeters to Inches 39
Feet to Meters...................... .3
Meters to Feet 3.28
Yards to Meters 91
Meters to Yards 1.09
Miles to Kilometers 1.61
Kilometers to Miles............ .62
1 Mile = 1.6 km
1 km = .62 Miles

WEIGHT

1 Ounce = .28 Grams
1 Pound = .4555 Kilograms
1 Gram = .04 Ounce
1 Kilogram = 2.2 Pounds

>TOURIST

TRAVEL QUESTIONS

- Do you bring presents home to family or friends after a vacation?
- Do you get motion sick?
- Do you have a favorite billboard?
- Do you know what to do if there is a flat tire?
- Do you like a sun roof open?
- Do you like to eat in the car?
- Do you like to wear sun glasses in the car?
- Do you like toppings on your ice cream?
- Do you use public bathrooms?
- Did you bring your cell phone and does it have power?
- Do you have a form of identification with you?
- Have you ever been pulled over by a cop?
- Have you ever given money to a stranger on a road trip?
- Have you ever taken a road trip with animals?
- Have you ever went on a vacation alone?
- Have you ever run out of gas?

- If you could move to any place in the world, where would it be?
- If you could travel anywhere in the world, where would you travel?
- If you could travel in any vehicle, which one would it be?
- If you had three things to wish for from a magic genie, what would they be?
- If you have a driver's license, how many times did it take you to pass the test?
- What are you the most afraid of on vacation?
- What do you want to get away from the most when you are on vacation?
- What foods smells bad to you?
- What item to you bring on ever trip with you away from home?
- What makes you sleepy?
- What song would you love to hear on the radio when you're cruising on the highway?
- What travel job would you want the least?
- What will you miss most while you are away from home?
- What is something you always wanted to try?

>TOURIST

- What is the best road side attraction that you ever saw?
- What is the farthest distance you ever biked?
- What is the farthest distance you ever walked?
- What is the weirdest thing you needed to buy while on vacation?
- What is your favorite candy?
- What is your favorite color car?
- What is your favorite family vacation?
- What is your favorite food in the world?
- What is your favorite gas station drink or food?
- What is your favorite license plate design?
- What is your favorite restaurant in the world?
- What is your favorite smell?
- What is your favorite song?
- What is your favorite sound that nature makes?
- What is your favorite thing to bring home from a vacation?
- What is your favorite vacation with friends?
- What is your favorite way to relax?

- What is your favorite weather conditions while driving?
- Where in the world would you rather never get to travel?
- Where is the farthest place you ever traveled in a car?
- Where is the farthest place you ever went North, South, East and West?
- Where is your favorite place in the world?
- Who is your favorite singer?
- Who taught you how to drive?
- Who will you miss the most while you are away?
- Who if the first person you will call when you get to your destination?
- Who brought you on your first vacation?
- Who likes to travel the most in your life?
- Would you rather be hot or cold?
- Would you rather drive above, below, or at the speed limited?
- Would you rather drive on a highway or a back road?
- Would you rather go on a train or a boat?
- Would you rather go to the beach or the woods?

>TOURIST

TRAVEL BUCKET LIST

1.

2.

3.

4.

5.

6.

7.

8.

9.

10.

>TOURIST

NOTES

Made in the USA
Las Vegas, NV
21 February 2025